MUSIC LESSONS
FOR ALEX

MUSIC LESSONS FOR ALEX

by
CAROLINE ARNOLD
photographs by
RICHARD HEWETT

CLARION BOOKS
TICKNOR & FIELDS : A HOUGHTON MIFFLIN COMPANY
NEW YORK

77 44

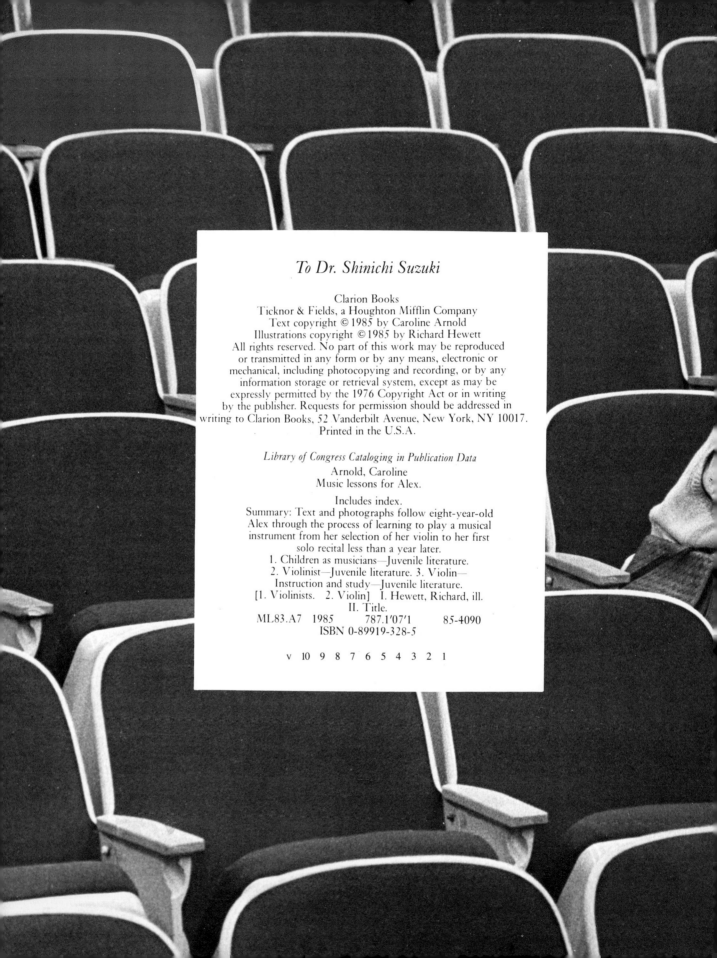

To Dr. Shinichi Suzuki

Clarion Books
Ticknor & Fields, a Houghton Mifflin Company
Text copyright © 1985 by Caroline Arnold
Illustrations copyright © 1985 by Richard Hewett

Library of Congress Cataloging in Publication Data
Arnold, Caroline
Music lessons for Alex.

Includes index.
Summary: Text and photographs follow eight-year-old
Alex through the process of learning to play a musical
instrument from her selection of her violin to her first
solo recital less than a year later.
1. Children as musicians—Juvenile literature.
2. Violinist—Juvenile literature. 3. Violin—
Instruction and study—Juvenile literature.
[1. Violinists. 2. Violin] I. Hewett, Richard, ill.
II. Title.
ML83.A7   1985   787.1′07′1   85-4090
ISBN 0-89919-328-5

v 10 9 8 7 6 5 4 3 2 1

The lights in the concert hall dimmed, and Alex and her family watched the musicians get ready to play. Then the conductor lifted his baton. Suddenly sounds from violins, violas, cellos, trumpets, clarinets, flutes, oboes, piano, and drums filled the room.

Alex could hardly take her eyes off the violinists. As they played, it seemed as if their fingers and bows almost danced across the violin strings.

When the concert was finished, everybody clapped.

"Oh, wasn't that beautiful!" said Alex. "I wish I could play the violin too."

"If you want to play the violin, you would need to take lessons," said Alex's father.

"And then you would need to practice," said Alex's mother.

"Yes," said Alex. "I want to take lessons. And I will practice every day."

During the next few weeks Alex's parents looked for a violin teacher in their community. They talked to the music teacher at Alex's school and to people they knew whose children already studied music. Finally they found a teacher they liked and arranged for Alex to begin lessons. Alex would take a thirty-minute lesson alone once a week. Every other week she would also go to a group lesson.

Before Alex could start lessons, she needed to get a violin. Alex and her mother went to a shop that rented and sold violins.

10

The teacher had suggested that they might like to rent a violin at first. "Some students," she had said, "buy their violins. But many students prefer to rent them until they stop growing or until they are sure they want to keep playing."

At the violin shop Alex tried several violins.

"Let's see which one is the best size for you," said Mr. Watanabe, the shopowner. "Your fingers should be able to reach the strings comfortably without your having to stretch your arm."

Alex found that a half-size violin was just right for her.

"What happens when I grow?" asked Alex.

"Then you will have to get a new violin," said Mr. Watanabe, "but that won't be for a year or so."

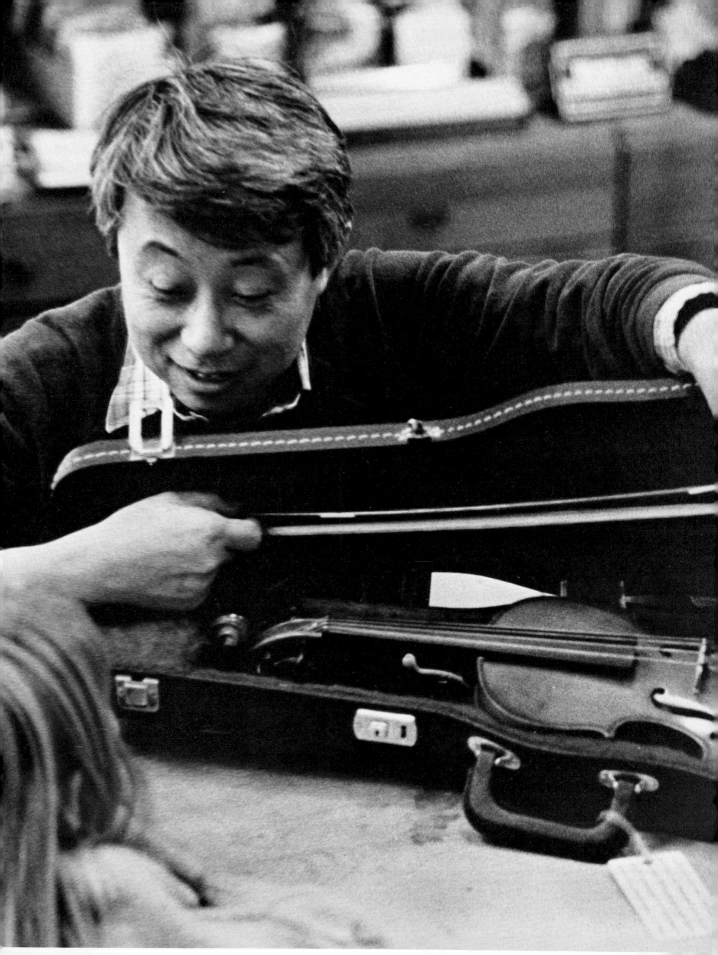

Then Mr. Watanabe helped Alex pick out a shoulder rest, a bow, and a case. "The case protects the violin," said Mr. Watanabe. "Always be sure to keep your violin and bow in it when you are not playing." Then Mr. Watanabe gave Alex a small box. "This is rosin for your bow," he said. "Your teacher will show you how to use it."

Alex could hardly wait for her first lesson.

The next day Alex and her mother went to the violin teacher's house.

"Hello," said the teacher. "You must be Alex. I'm Mrs. Weisner. Your mother can sit on the sofa and listen, and you can come over here."

Alex got out her violin. "Can I start to play now?" she asked.

"Not yet," said Mrs. Weisner. "First we have to get everything ready. Most instruments have to be adjusted in some way before you can play them. Stringed instruments like violins, violas, and cellos need to be tuned. The strings on the violin should sound like the notes E, A, D, and G."

"How do I know if the strings are in tune?" asked Alex.

"You can use a tuning fork or pitch pipe, or you can match the sounds to the same notes on a piano."

Mrs. Weisner pulled the bow across the A string of Alex's violin while Alex played the A above middle C on the piano. They did not sound quite the same. "If the sound is too high, then we turn the peg to loosen the string," said Mrs. Weisner. "If it is too low, we tighten the string. The tighter the string, the higher the sound. If you have screws at the other end of the strings, you can turn them to make fine adjustments."

Finally the violin was in tune. "Can I play now?" asked Alex.

16

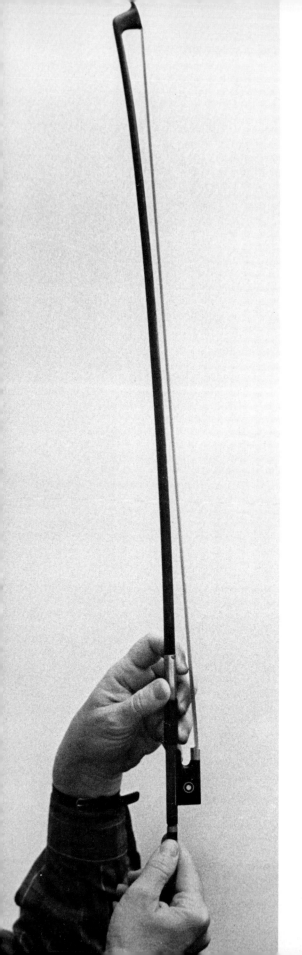

"Not yet," said Mrs. Weisner. "Now we must get your bow ready." She showed Alex how to turn the knob at the end of the bow to tighten the bow hair. Then she pulled the bow hair across the cake of rosin. "The rosin is sticky and keeps the bow from slipping," said Mrs. Weisner.

"Can I play now?" asked Alex.

"Almost," said Mrs. Weisner, "but now *you* have to get ready." Mrs. Weisner had Alex stand on a piece of paper. "When you stand to play, your feet should be slightly apart, like this. Your weight should fall evenly on each foot," said Mrs. Weisner. Then she drew around Alex's shoes. "You can take this paper home with you," said Mrs. Weisner. "It will remind you how to place your feet if you forget."

"When I was at the concert," said Alex, "everyone sat down to play."

"Yes," said Mrs. Weisner. "You can learn to do that later. However, whether you sit or stand, it is important to have good balance."

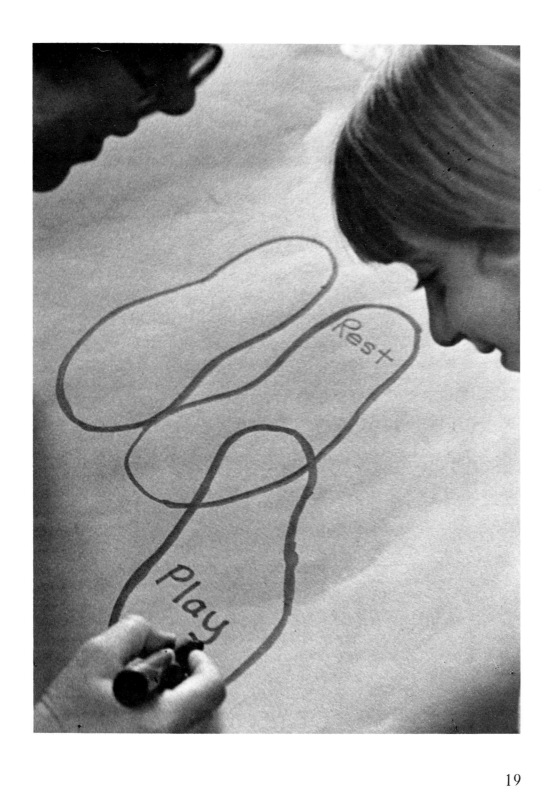

19

Alex then put the violin on her left shoulder. She tried to hold it straight and steady.

"It feels funny," said Alex.

"I know," said Mrs. Weisner, "but you will get used to it. It is important to have a good hold on the violin with your chin so that the fingers of your left hand will be free to play the notes. You can test your chin hold by letting go with your hand."

Alex let go.

"Good!" said Mrs. Weisner. "If you are sure you have a good grip, you can try spreading your arms like wings."

"Look!" said Alex. "I can do it!"

"Very good," said Mrs. Weisner. "Put your hand back on the violin and we will begin to play."

"Do I need music?" asked Alex.

"Not today," said Mrs. Weisner. "Some teachers give their students music to read from the very first lesson, but I prefer to wait until you have learned some other things first. You do not have to be able to read music to play music."

Mrs. Weisner showed Alex how to hold the bow and how to pull it across the E and A strings. She then played a simple rhythm on each string. The rhythm had four quick bow strokes and two longer ones.

"A good way to remember the rhythm," said Mrs. Weisner, "is to think of the words 'Mississippi River.' You say 'Mississippi' with four quick sounds and 'River' with two slower sounds."

22

Alex tried playing as Mrs. Weisner said "Mississippi" during the four quick notes and "River" during the two long ones.

"Yes," said Alex, "that makes it easier."

Soon Alex's first lesson was over.

"What should I practice at home?" asked Alex.

"Do all the things we did at the lesson today," said Mrs. Weisner. "Also, here is a tape of the pieces you will be learning. Listen to it each day. Careful listening is just as important as careful playing. It trains your ears to hear each note in tune. Then you will learn to match your playing to that on the tape."

"How long should I practice each day?" asked Alex.

"It's like any other skill. The more you practice, the faster you will progress. Probably it will take you about thirty minutes to do everything you learned today," said Mrs. Weisner. "When you become more advanced, it will take longer. However, the time you spend is not so important as how you practice. Practicing well for a short time is better than sloppy practicing for a long time."

At home during the next week Alex practiced every day. She stood in front of a mirror to check her posture. She listened to the tape, and she practiced the "Mississippi River" rhythm.

When Alex practiced the rhythm, she tried to make a good clear sound the way that Mrs. Weisner had showed her. She tried to pull the bow across just one string at a time. But it was hard to do that and keep the bow moving in a straight line. Sometimes it made a terrible scratchy sound.

"Eek!" said Alex's sister, Kate. "That sounds awful!"

"I know," said Alex. "It looks so easy when other people play."

Alex had never thought there would be so many things to learn about playing the violin. Somehow, before she had started lessons, she had imagined that after a few weeks she would be playing all sorts of pieces. Now she realized that it was going to take a long time just to learn even her first piece.

26

At Alex's next lesson she showed Mrs. Weisner how well she had learned everything.

"Very good," said Mrs. Weisner. "You have improved a lot since last week."

"Yes," said Alex, "but this doesn't sound like real music. When will I learn my first piece?"

Mrs. Weisner smiled. "Soon," she promised.

Mrs. Weisner showed Alex how to press the first finger of her left hand down on the E string about an inch from the end. Alex tried playing on the E string with her finger down.

"When you play a string without putting any fingers down, it is called an open string," said Mrs. Weisner. "Now you know three notes—open A, open E, and your first finger on the E string."

Alex tried playing those three notes in a row. Then she tried playing them in the "Mississippi River" rhythm.

"What does that sound like?" asked Mrs. Weisner.

Alex smiled. "It sounds like the beginning of 'Twinkle, Twinkle, Little Star.' That's the first song on my tape!"

"That's right," said Mrs. Weisner. "Does that sound like 'real music'?"

"Yes," said Alex, and she played it again.

Alex tried so hard to play the notes that she forgot to stand correctly.

"Be careful," said Mrs. Weisner. "If your violin droops, it is hard to pull your bow the right way."

Alex's lesson was almost over, and two other students were waiting for their lesson to begin. Mrs. Weisner asked them to get out their violins.

"Good posture needs practice just like good playing," said Mrs. Weisner to Alex. "Cyrus and Feroz can show you a game that helps you to practice good posture."

Alex and Mrs. Weisner counted to ten while Feroz and Cyrus each tried to balance a Ping-Pong ball between the D and G strings. Twice they had to start over when one of the violins tipped and the ball fell to the floor.

"You can try this game at home," Mrs. Weisner suggested to Alex. "See how high you can count before the ball drops."

Later that week Alex, Cyrus, and Feroz went to their group lessons in a building nearby. Students of several teachers attended the lessons. They could all play together because at their private lessons they all studied the same music.

Each class was taught by a different teacher. Although Mrs. Weisner taught classes at the group lessons, Alex's group was taught by someone else.

The students in each class were all at about the same level. Alex was in the beginners class. While she was waiting for her

violin to be tuned, she made friends with a girl named Monica. Then the class began.

First the students all played the "Mississippi River" rhythm together. Then Alex and the other children listened while the teacher clapped a different rhythm. It sounded like the rhythm of the words "ice cream and applesauce." Then they all clapped it together. They tried this with several other new rhythms.

"At home you can play this game with a friend," said the teacher, "and each of you can take turns making up new rhythms."

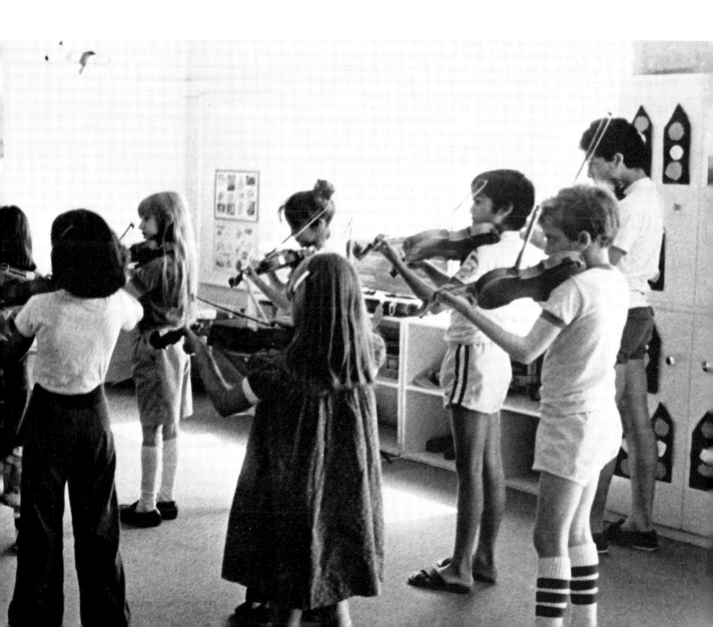

Then the children put down their violins and held just their bows.

"Can you pretend your fingers are a spider?" asked the teacher.

Alex wiggled her fingers like a spider.

"Let's see if your spider fingers can climb up to the top of the bow like this," said the teacher.

All the children tried to make their fingers climb. It wasn't as easy as it looked.

"This exercise makes your fingers strong," said the teacher, "and helps you to have a good bow hold."

They played some more, and soon the class was over. It was time for Alex to go to her music-reading class.

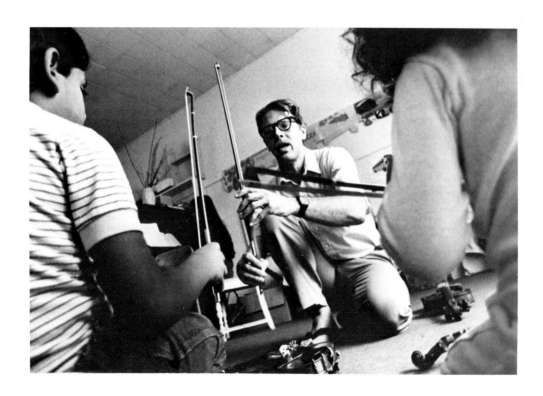

All the children who attended the group lessons went to two classes each time—one to practice playing and another to practice reading. Children who had begun to read music worked in simple music books. Beginning students like Alex started with reading games. Alex learned that music is usually written on five lines called a staff. Each line and space on the staff has a name, just like the names of the notes on the violin and piano. Alex learned that when the notes go up on the staff, they sound higher. When they go down, they sound lower.

36

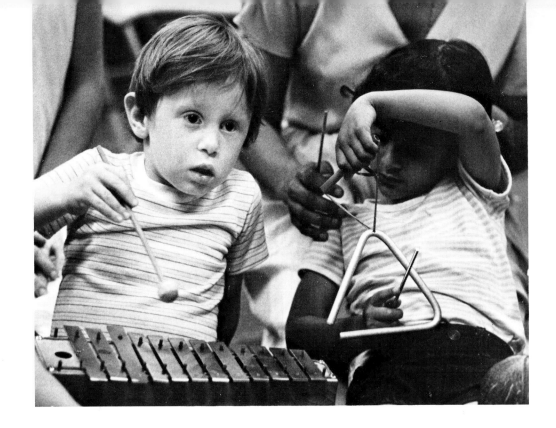

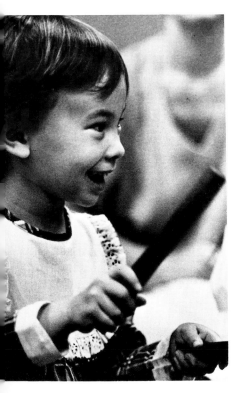

During the reading time the smallest children at the group lessons, who were too young to read, went to other rooms. There they played rhythm games. The teacher gave them triangles, drums, cymbals, and other rhythm instruments. They clanged, banged, or tapped their instruments to help the teacher tell a story.

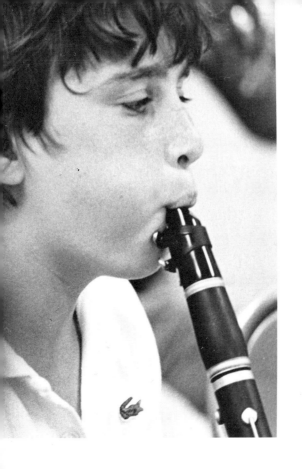

The most advanced students, who could already read music well, played in small groups or in a string orchestra. Some of the children at the group lessons also played in the orchestras at their schools.

At Feroz and Cyrus's school the orchestra met for an hour once a week. Like Cyrus and Feroz, many of the students took private music lessons as well. But others had learned to play in group lessons at school and did not have a private teacher.

Each week the orchestra teacher gave the students music to learn at home. In school, when they practiced together, the students arranged their chairs and music stands so that they could watch their music and the orchestra teacher at the same time. "Remember," the teacher would say, "to listen to one another and to watch me. If we do not all start and stop at the same time, it just sounds like noise—not beautiful music!"

Alex was not yet ready to play in her school orchestra.

The weeks went by quickly as Alex continued her lessons. Each week Mrs. Weisner taught her something new. Alex learned how to use her other fingers to make other notes. She learned how to make loud and soft sounds with different kinds of bowing. Gradually she learned all the notes to the first song on her tape. At home she practiced hard to try to make her notes sound just like the ones on the tape. Finally she could play the whole song from beginning to end.

"Listen to me!" she said to Mrs. Weisner at her next lesson, "I can play all of 'Twinkle, Twinkle, Little Star.'"

"Wonderful!" said Mrs. Weisner.

Each week, if Alex had prepared her lesson well, Mrs. Weisner let her choose a sticker to take home. This week Alex chose an extra-special one.

"Look," she said to her mother after she got home, "this is my sticker for learning my first piece."

42

At the next lesson Mrs. Weisner gave Alex her first music books.

"Oh, this looks hard," said Alex. "I'll never learn what all these funny lines and dots mean."

"Yes, you will," said Mrs. Weisner. "You've already learned what some of these are at the group lessons. Remember when you were first learning to read words in books? You didn't learn everything all at once. First you learned to read letters, then you learned to read sounds and words, and only after that did you learn to read sentences. It will be like that with music too. You will learn one thing at a time."

As the weeks went by, Alex found that reading music became easier. Over the next few months she learned new pieces in the book and practiced them at home and at the group lessons.

As Alex learned how to read music, she liked to go ahead in her book and learn new pieces. In many ways they were much more fun to play than her old pieces. Mrs. Weisner sometimes had to warn Alex to slow down a bit.

"Don't be in such a hurry," said Mrs. Weisner. "If you go on to the new pieces before you have learned everything you can from your old ones, you miss some important points. You may also develop sloppy playing habits, and it's much harder to get rid of bad habits than to learn to play right the first time."

Mrs. Weisner also encouraged Alex to keep playing the pieces she had already learned.

"As you become a better musician, you will play your earlier pieces better and better," said Mrs. Weisner. "No matter how well you play a piece, there is almost always some way that you can still work to improve it."

At home Alex divided her practice time into four parts—old pieces, new pieces, reading, and listening.

Sometimes Alex's friends called when Alex was practicing. They would ask if Alex could come out and play.

"Not now," Alex would say, "I have to practice."

At times like these Alex wished she didn't have to practice every day. Sometimes she even thought of quitting lessons.

"It's hard," said Alex to Mrs. Weisner at her next lesson. "I really want to learn to play the violin, but sometimes I just don't feel like practicing."

"I know," said Mrs. Weisner. "Everybody feels that way sometimes—even professional musicians—and they practice many hours every day."

"Do I really have to practice *every* day?" asked Alex.

"It's all right if you skip practicing one day each week," said Mrs. Weisner. "However, it's important to practice regularly. Then you don't forget what you've learned from one time to the next."

"What can I do to make my practicing easier?" asked Alex.

"Well," said Mrs. Weisner, "it helps to have a regular practice time each day. Some people like to make a list of each thing they need to do. Other people like to use a clock or a timer to know exactly how long they have to practice."

Mrs. Weisner got out two cans and some small pieces of paper. "Here's a game you can play to help you practice." On each piece of paper she wrote one thing Alex needed to practice. Then she put all the papers in a can marked "Do It" and held it up for Alex to pick one out.

Alex read what the paper said and did it.

"Now put the paper in the can that says 'Done It,'" said Mrs. Weisner. "Each day you can do this until the 'Do It' can is empty. Then you will be done practicing."

"That's fun," said Alex, "and I'll never know what is coming next."

"Another way to make practicing fun is to do it with a friend," suggested Mrs. Weisner. "You can play together or take turns listening to each other. You might even try playing two on a violin. It's fun and helps to develop your coordination."

"Yes," said Alex. "I'll try that with Monica."

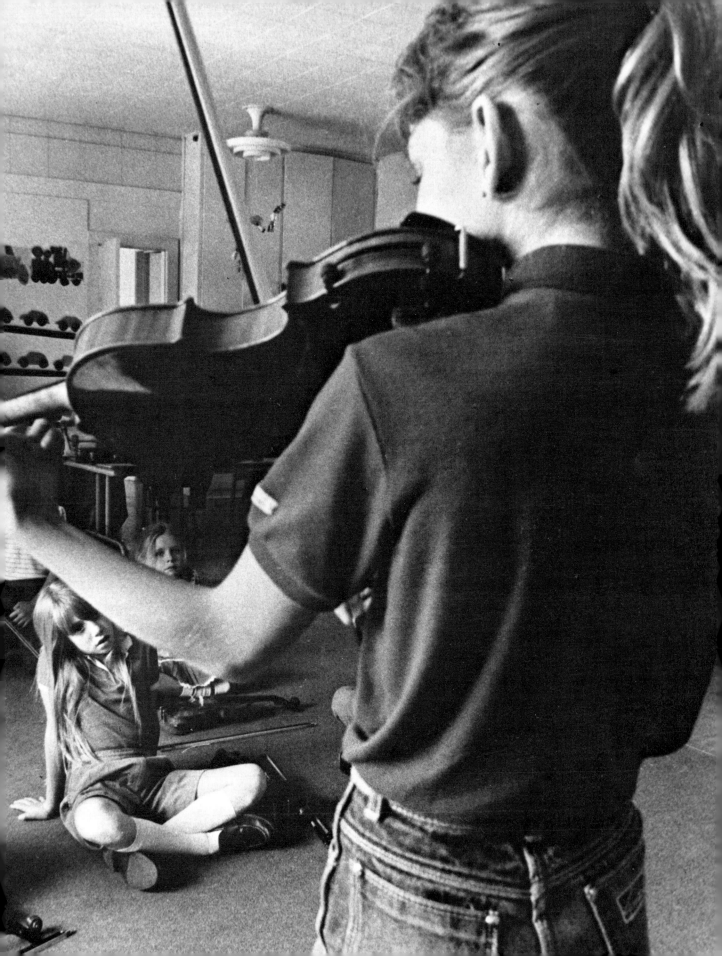

When Alex and Monica went to the next group lesson, each student had a chance to play alone in front of the group. They learned that at the end of the school year everyone would play a piece in a recital for all the students and their families and friends.

At the next lesson Mrs. Weisner helped Alex choose a recital piece. Alex would have several weeks to get ready to perform.

"When you prepare a piece to perform," said Mrs. Weisner, "it's like polishing a piece of silver. Before you start, it is partly shiny, but there are also some dull spots. Polishing will make it sparkle all over.

"One way to find parts that need polishing is to record your playing," said Mrs. Weisner, "and then listen to it. It's easier to hear mistakes when you are not playing at the same time."

At the next lesson Mrs. Weisner showed Alex how to play with a metronome to make sure she kept her rhythm steady. The metronome was like a loud clock. Its regular clicks kept a steady beat, but unlike a clock, the clicks could be made to go faster or slower. "It's easy to slow down or speed up while you are playing," said Mrs. Weisner, "and the metronome will show you where you might be doing this. If you don't have a metronome, you can get someone to clap a steady beat while you play."

Each day at home Alex chose one part of her recital piece on which to work especially hard. Her sister, Kate, sometimes helped her by playing the piano so Alex could hear if her notes were perfectly in tune.

At the recital there would be a professional accompanist to play with each student. "Don't worry about keeping up with the accompanist," said Mrs. Weisner. "You are the soloist, and the accompanist's job is to keep up with you."

"What if I make a mistake?" asked Alex.

"If you do make a small mistake, try to just keep going. Most people in the audience probably won't even notice. But if you do stumble over a few notes, then the accompanist will adjust. However, if you are well prepared, which I know you will be, then you won't make any big mistakes."

Alex was not so sure. She had practiced her piece well, but this was her first recital. During the past nine months she had played at home for her friends and grandparents, but never before such a large group. Alex was excited, but she was also a little bit scared.

"Don't worry," said Alex's mother. "I know you will do well, and we are all looking forward to hearing you."

On the day of the recital Alex took a bath, washed her hair, and put on a pretty dress.

The recital was being given in the auditorium of the same building where Alex went for group lessons. When Alex and her family arrived, Alex got out her violin and had it tuned. Then she went backstage. The printed program showed when it would be her turn to play.

One at a time each student walked onto the stage and played his or her piece. When it was finished, the student bowed and the audience clapped.

Soon it was Alex's turn.

Alex walked onto the stage and faced the audience. She could see her mother and father and Kate smiling at her. Then she put her violin on her shoulder, lifted her bow, and began to play.

The accompanist followed Alex, and the notes seemed to flow one right after the other. When she came to the end of the piece, everyone clapped, and Alex bowed. Alex smiled. A year ago she had not even known how to hold a violin, and now she had learned to make beautiful music.

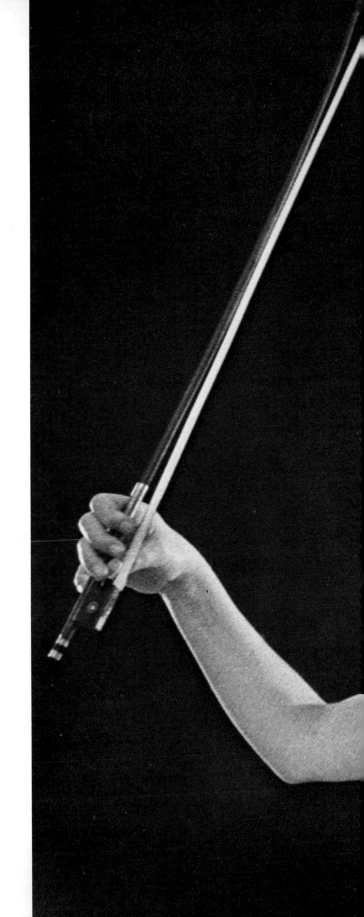

ACKNOWLEDGMENTS

We want to thank everyone whose cheerful cooperation helped to make this book possible, and we are especially grateful to Alex, Kate, Elizabeth, and Michael Vittes and to Susan Weisner. Many thanks also to Dr. David Avshalomov, Kyozo Watanabe, Idell Low, the students and teachers of the San Fernando Valley California Suzuki Program, and the students of the Brentwood Science Magnet School, Los Angeles, California.

INDEX

Accompanists, 54, 61
Alex and the violin
  desire to play, 7-8
  eagerness for new pieces, 46
    advice to master old ones, 45
  finding a music teacher, 8
  finding a violin, 8-13
    buying or renting, 11
  first music books, 45
  first song learned, 42
  music lessons, 8, 15-25, 28-31, 42,
    45
    group lessons, 8, 32-34, 45
    music-reading classes, 34, 36-39
  recital
    performing, 59-61
    preparing for, 53-57

Bow (violin), 13, 16, 18, 22, 34

Concert hall, in the, 7
Cyrus, 30-31, 32, 41

Feroz, 30-31, 32, 41
Fingering, 28, 42
Foot position and balance, 18

Group lessons, 8, 32-34, 45
  finger-strengthening exercises, 34
  playing alone for group, 53

Kate, 26, 54, 59

Metronome, 53
Monica, 32, 53
Music, how to read, 36, 45
Music lessons, 8, 15-25, 28-31, 42,
    45
  fingering, 28, 42
  holding and using the bow, 22, 42
  holding the violin properly, 20
  listening to music, importance of,
    23, 28
  posture (stance and balance), 18,
    28-31
  preparing the bow, 18
  rhythm, 22-23, 28
  tuning the violin, 15-16
  see also Group lessons; Music-
    reading classes
Music-reading classes, 34, 36-39
Music teacher, finding a, 8

Open strings, 28
Orchestras, student, 41

Posture (stance and balance), 18, 25,
    28-31
Practice at home, 23-26, 45
    posture, 30-31
    rhythms, 33
    so much to learn, 26
    value and necessity of, 48-51
        establish regularity, 51
        make a game of it, 50-51
        play with a friend, 51

Recital
    performing, 59-61
    preparing for, 53-57
Rhythm, 22-23, 25, 28, 33, 53

Rhythm instruments, 39
Rosin, 13, 18

Staff (music), 36

Tuning the violin, 15-16

Violinists, 7
Violins, 8
    accessories for, 13
    the bow, 13, 16, 18, 22
    buying or renting, 11
    holding properly, 20
    strings, 15-16
    tuning, 15-16

Watanabe, Mr. 11-13
Weisner, Mrs., 15-25, 26, 28-31, 32,
    42, 45, 46, 48-51, 53, 54